THE SHARK
ATTACK
FILES

Thanks to the creative team:
Senior Editor: Alice Peebles
Fact Checking: Tom Jackson
Illustration: Jeremy Pyke
Picture Research: Nic Dean
Design: Perfect Bound Ltd

Hungry Tomato®
A division of Lerner Publishing Group, Inc.
241 First Avenue North
Minneapolis, MN 55401 USA

For reading levels and more information, look up this title at
www.lernerbooks.com.

Main body text set in Scene Std Regular 10/13.
Typeface provided by Monotype Typography.

Library of Congress Cataloging-in-Publication Data

Names: Mason, Paul, 1967– author.
Title: The shark attack files / Paul Mason.
Description: Minneapolis : Hungry Tomato, [2018] | Series:
Wild world of sharks | Audience: Ages 8-12. | Audience:
Grades 4 to 6.
Identifiers: LCCN 2017029843 (print) | LCCN 2017025401
(ebook) | ISBN 9781512498806 (eb pdf) | ISBN
9781512459784 (lb : alk. paper)
Subjects: LCSH: Shark attacks—Juvenile literature. |
Sharks—Behavior—Juvenile literature. | Sharks—
Territoriality—Juvenile literature.
Classification: LCC QL638.93 (print) | LCC QL638.93 .M38
2018 (ebook) | DDC
597.31566--dc23
LC record available at https://lccn.loc.gov/2017029843

Manufactured in the United States of America
1-43038-27706-8/14/2017

THE SHARK ATTACK FILES

by Paul Mason

HUNGRY
TOMATO®
Minneapolis

CONTENTS

SHARK ATTACKS: THE REALITY

For most people, the thought of being attacked by a shark is terrifying. Fortunately, though, shark attacks are extremely rare.

The Chances of Being Bitten

Most sharks are harmless. You are far more likely to have a car crash on your way to the beach than to be bitten by a shark when you get there. Even being struck by lightning is more likely.

There are about **450 different shark species. Of these:**

Only **13 species** (2.9 percent) are suspected of having killed humans.

Most sharks are harmless, but in some places there is a risk of meeting dangerous ones. This sign on a California beach warns people of fatal shark attacks that have happened here in the past.

WARNING
(¡Precaución!)
FATAL
SHARK ATTACKS
(Ataque de Tiburon Fatal)
SWIM/SURF AT
YOUR OWN RISK
(Nade bajo su propio riesgo)

KEEP AWAY FROM MARINE WILDLIFE
(No se acerque a los animales marinos)

Identifying the Attacker

Only great white, bull, and tiger sharks are known to have ever killed more than 10 people. But it is not always certain what kind of shark is the **perpetrator** of an attack. Oceanic whitetip sharks are thought to have killed many shipwrecked sailors (see pages 8–9). But without surviving witnesses, oceanic whitetips cannot be included in shark attack statistics.

Only **seven species** (1.6 percent) are thought to have killed more than one person.

Only **three species** (0.67 percent) are known to have killed more than 10 people.

The great white shark is the world's most dangerous species. Even so, great whites are thought to have killed fewer than one person per year over the last 100 years.

Shark Science: Shark I.D.

Experts can sometimes identify what kind of shark attacked someone from the bite marks. Different shark species have different-shaped jaws. Their teeth are also arranged in a special way. This all means that a shark's bite mark is like a simple fingerprint.

THE JERSEY SHORE MAN-EATER

New York

Date: July 1–12, 1916
Location: New Jersey Coastline

Matawan ✕
July 12

Spring Lake ✕
July 6

Philadelphia

Beach Haven
July 1
✕

In 1916, shark attacks off the East Coast of the United States left four people dead. The attacks marked the beginning of our modern terror of sharks.

ATTACK 1: BEACH HAVEN

On Saturday, July 1, vacationer Charles Vansant decided to go for a swim before dinner. Soon after entering the water, Vansant began shouting for help. A large shark had attacked his legs. A lifeguard and another man pulled him to shore followed by the shark, but within minutes Vansant had died.

ATTACK 2: SPRING LAKE

Five days after Vansant's death, Charles Bruder was swimming about 320 feet (100 m) offshore when he too was attacked. There was so much blood in the water that a woman told lifeguards she thought a red canoe had capsized. The lifeguards rowed out to help, but Bruder died on the way back to land.

The location of the 1916 shark attacks along the East Coast of the United States.

ATTACKS 3, 4, AND 5: MATAWAN

Six days after the Spring Lake attack, sea captain Thomas Cottrell spotted a shark in Matawan Creek. He tried to warn people, but they did not believe sharks swam in rivers. Minutes later, 11-year-old Lester Stilwell was attacked and killed by the shark. When townspeople went to find Lester's body, Watson Fisher was also attacked and later died.

About a half hour later Joseph Dunn was swimming off a dock with friends when word of the attacks reached them. As he climbed out of the water, the shark bit his leg. After a tug of war between his friends and the shark, Joseph was pulled from the water and survived.

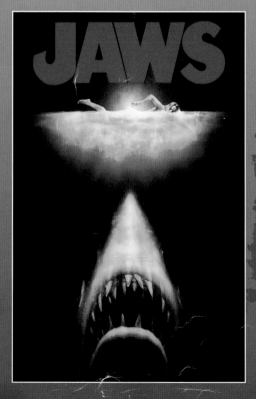

The hit 1975 movie Jaws, about a killer shark off the coast of Long Island, was inspired by the Jersey Shore man-eater.

SHARK SCIENCE: WHICH SHARK LAUNCHED THE ATTACKS?

It is not certain what species carried out the Jersey Shore attacks. There are two main suspects:

- A bull shark (bull sharks regularly swim in fresh water)
- A young great white

On July 14, two days after the last attacks, an 8-foot 10-inch (2.7 m) great white was caught and killed close to Matawan Creek. The attacks stopped, making it likely that this was the shark responsible.

THE INDIANAPOLIS SHIPWRECK

Just after midnight, the US Navy ship *Indianapolis* was sunk by torpedoes from a Japanese submarine. About 900 of the crew ended up in the water, drifting in groups in their life jackets.

The oceanic whitetip grows to 13 feet (4 m) and weighs up to 370 pounds (170 kg).

SECRET MISSION

The *Indianapolis* had been on a secret mission. It had delivered an atomic bomb, which in a few days would be used to attack the Japanese city of Hiroshima. The mission was so secret that it was days before rescue arrived. As the shipwrecked sailors waited, sharks began to gather and attack them.

Long pectoral fins give the whitetip part of its Latin name: longimanus or "long hands." The shark's English name comes from the white tips on its fins.

Rescued survivors from the USS Indianapolis *receive medical help on the island of Guam.*

The oceanic whitetip, a strong, thick-bodied shark, is thought to have attacked the crew of the Indianapolis.

CAUTIOUS BUT DETERMINED

Oceanic whitetips are cautious hunters, especially when attacking large prey. If they come close to investigate, it may be possible to beat them away. The danger has not gone away, though. Whitetips continue to shadow or circle their prey until another opportunity to attack occurs.

Nearly 900 crew members survived the initial sinking of the *Indianapolis*. Many then died from exposure and dehydration, as well as from shark attacks. Only 321 were rescued alive, and only 317 of them survived. No one is certain how many of the dead were eaten by sharks, but it is thought to have been at least 150 people.

The powerful jaw has wide triangular teeth above for slicing into prey and smaller pointed teeth below for a good grip.

SHARK SCIENCE: WHAT CAUSED THE ATTACK

Oceanic whitetip sharks usually hunt alone, but they are known to gather quickly at possible food sources—including shipwrecks.

Any oceanic whitetips within a few kilometers were attracted by the noise of a ship going down. As they swim nearer, the sharks began to smell the sailors in the water. Once they were really close, the sharks could see their victims.

SPEARFISHER RODNEY FOX

Date: December 8, 1963
Location: Aldinga Beach, South Australia

Rodney Fox was spearfishing far from shore when he was attacked by a great white shark. He somehow survived— which most experts agree was a miracle.

A great white shark patrols the ocean, looking for prey.

THE CONTEST

Rodney was taking part in a spearfishing contest. As defending champion, he was determined to win again. To do this, Rodney needed to spear unusual fish, so he set off for some rocks about 60 feet (18 m) below the surface. He spotted a Dusky Morwong—a fish worth big points—but did not see a nearby great white.

THE ATTACK

The shark attacked Rodney. It hit him so hard, he later said it felt like being struck by a train. It grabbed him around the chest, but Rodney fought back, poking the shark in the eye, and it let him go. He tried to push the shark away but accidentally put his hand in its mouth.

Rodney swam back to the surface, but as he looked down, he saw a chilling sight: "This great big shark coming up with its mouth wide open."

At the last second, the shark turned and grabbed the fish Rodney had speared. They were on a rope tied to his belt and he was dragged underwater . . . but the rope snapped, and Rodney made it back to the surface. By now a boat had come to the scene, and he was pulled on board and rushed to the hospital.

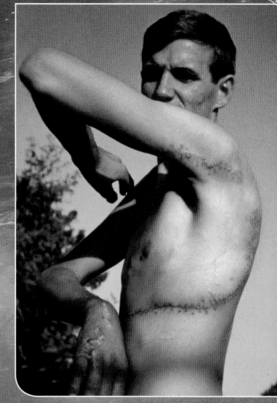

Rodney Fox displays the scars from the great white's attack. He needed 462 stitches in his body and 92 in his hand and arm.

SHARK SCIENCE: WHAT CAUSED THE ATTACK

There were three main reasons for the attack on Rodney Fox:

- The seas of South Australia are home to a lot of great whites.
- After four hours of the spearfishing contest, a trail of blood had been released for sharks to follow.
- Speared fish wriggle in a way that also attracts sharks.

AFTER THE ATTACK

Once he had recovered, Rodney became fascinated by great white sharks. He invented **cage diving** as a way of safely seeing them in their own environment. In 2001, he started the Fox Shark Research Foundation. He is now one of the world's leading experts on the great white.

SHARK EXPERT ERICH RITTER

Date: April 11, 2002
Location: Bahamas, Caribbean Sea

Shark expert Dr. Erich Ritter had a theory about shark attacks. He thought that sharks were attracted by fast human heartbeats. Therefore, he believed lowering your heartbeat would keep you safe.

THEORY IN ACTION

Ritter regularly swam with bull sharks or stood chest-deep in water where they were feeding. He used special exercises to slow down his breathing and heartbeat. Bull sharks are among the most aggressive, dangerous sharks. Ritter was sometimes **bumped** by the sharks and had to leave the water, but until 2002, he had never been bitten.

Bull sharks have attacked humans at least 100 times. They get their name from their short snouts, fierce nature, and habit of butting victims before biting.

At Carbrook golf course in Australia, balls lost in the water stay lost! Bull sharks patrol the lake, having first swum there during a flood and become trapped.

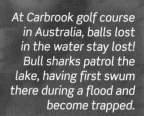

BULL SHARK

RITTER BITTEN

In 2002, Dr. Ritter was explaining his theory to a TV presenter. The two men were standing waist-deep in water, surrounded by bull sharks. To show how well the theory worked, raw fish had been put in the water for the sharks to feed on. Unfortunately, a short time into the interview one of the sharks bit Dr. Ritter on the lower leg.

Ritter and the interviewer quickly got out of the water, and Ritter was rushed to a hospital. He survived, but spent weeks in the hospital and lost a large piece of his calf. He is unlikely ever to be able to use his foot properly again because the shark bit off so much muscle.

SHARK SCIENCE: WHAT CAUSED THE ATTACK

Some shark experts had feared Dr. Ritter would eventually be bitten. They thought this for two main reasons:

1) Deliberately spending a lot of time in the water with dangerous sharks makes an attack more likely.

2) Dr. Ritter went into the water with bare legs. Underwater, skin can look similar to a light-colored fish. Hungry, curious sharks are attracted to this color, and they may take a bite to see if it's food.

SURFER BETHANY HAMILTON

Date: October 31, 2003
Location: Hawaii, Pacific Ocean

One October morning in 2003, 13-year-old Bethany Hamilton went surfing off Tunnels Beach in Hawaii with her friend, Alana Blanchard, Alana's brother, and her father, Holt.

THE ATTACK

The surfers paddled out into the warm Hawaiian waters to catch some fun waves. At around 7:30 a.m., Bethany was lying on her surfboard with her left arm dangling in the water. Seconds later, a shark had bitten her arm off. It happened so fast that none of the other surfers in the water even noticed.

THE RESCUE

Holt Blanchard knew that many shark-attack victims bleed to death. He used his surfboard **leash** as a **tourniquet** to slow Bethany's bleeding. The surfers then began the long 650-foot (200 m) paddle back to shore, which they managed in safety.

Bethany was rushed to a hospital. There, in a strange coincidence, her father was waiting for an operation. Bethany took her dad's place on the operating table. The wound was closed up, and, despite losing 60 percent of her blood, Bethany survived.

Bethany Hamilton was attacked by a tiger shark like this one. Tiger sharks haunt warm, tropical waters.

In 2011, a film called Soul Surfer was released. It tells the story of the attack on Bethany and her return to surfing. The film is based on Bethany's book of the same name, which came out in 2004.

AFTER THE ATTACK

Soon after the attack, a group of fishermen caught a 14-foot (4.3 m) tiger shark close by. Experts compared the shark's mouth with the bite marks on Bethany's surfboard. It was the shark that had attacked her.

Once she had recovered, Bethany got back on her surfboard. Since then, she has won the NSSA National Competition, as well as contests at Pipeline, Hawaii—one of the world's toughest waves.

She may have lost her arm to a shark in 2003, but Bethany Hamilton still rips! Here she is competing in a surfing contest in Hawaii in 2008.

SHARK SCIENCE: WHAT CAUSED THE ATTACK

Reports said that when Bethany was attacked, there were sea turtles in the water. Tiger sharks hunt turtles, so they may have attracted this particular shark.

Once there, the shark saw the surfer's light-colored arm in the water. It probably bit her thinking her arm was a fish.

SURFER ELIO CANESTRI

Date: April 12, 2015
Location: Réunion, Indian Ocean

Taking to the water around the island of Réunion poses a huge risk. Between 1996 and 2015, there were 28 shark attacks there. In 14 of the attacks, the victim died.

ATTACKS ON RÉUNION

After five people had died in just two years, the authorities decided they had to do something. In 2013 swimming and surfing were banned on many of the island's beaches. In 2014, there was only one attack, and the surfer escaped with minor injuries. But in February 2015, a swimmer was killed close to shore. All water activities were banned unless there was a shark spotter on the lookout.

BULL SHARK

THE ATTACK ON ELIO

On April 12, 2015, 13-year-old Elio Canestri paddled out with his friends at a surf spot called Zaigrettes. The surfers were about 160 feet (50 m) from shore when a wave came Elio's way. As he paddled to catch it, a bull shark attacked. Although a rescue boat quickly reached him, Elio did not survive. He was the seventh person to be killed by Réunion's sharks in just four years.

Bull sharks are thought to be behind almost all the attacks in the seas off Réunion.

PROTESTS IN RÉUNION

After Elio's death there were protests about people being killed in shark attacks. Two beaches were **netted** to make them safe for surfers and swimmers. Underwater lookouts armed with harpoon guns were posted. Even so, attacks have continued. By 2017, three more surfers had been attacked but survived. Then in February 2017, yet another surfer was killed by a shark.

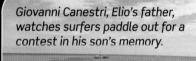

Giovanni Canestri, Elio's father, watches surfers paddle out for a contest in his son's memory.

SHARK SCIENCE: WHAT CAUSED THE ATTACKS

No one is sure why Réunion has seen so many shark attacks. There are several possible explanations:

- A new marine park created in 2007 has boosted fish numbers, so there is more for sharks to eat.
- The sale of shark meat has been banned, which means sharks are no longer caught.
- The number of reef sharks, which used to eat many of the young bull sharks, has fallen.

ATTACKS IN NORTHERN CALIFORNIA

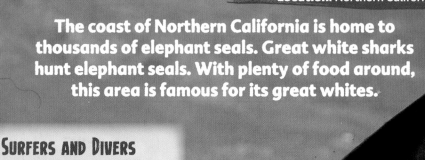

Date: September 15-30, 1984
Location: Northern California, Pacific Ocean

The coast of Northern California is home to thousands of elephant seals. Great white sharks hunt elephant seals. With plenty of food around, this area is famous for its great whites.

SURFERS AND DIVERS

The seals and sharks are not alone in California's seas. The state has great surfing waves and rich ocean life. It is popular with surfers and divers, especially spearfishers. Over the years there have been many shark attacks in Northern California.

During the breeding season, from January to March, there are thousands of elephant seals for sharks to hunt.

Omar Conger

On September 15, 1984, Omar Conger was out diving for **abalone** with his friend Chris Rehm. They were on the surface when, as Chris later said:

> *"[A] huge white shark came up, grabbed [Omar] from behind, and while shaking him violently, pulled him under the water. I never saw the shark before the attack."*

Chris pulled his friend on to a **surf mat** they had been using and swam to shore, all the time expecting the shark to reappear. They reached shore without seeing it again, but Omar had died.

Paul Parsons

Two weeks after Omar Conger died, Paul Parsons was diving for abalone. When he was underwater, he felt scared without knowing why, so he came back to the surface. His boat was 320 feet (100 m) away, so Paul decided it would be safer on the bottom and dived back down. When he surfaced a second time to get into the boat, a shark attacked. Paul fought until it released him and was hauled into the boat. He was badly bitten but made a full recovery.

SHARK SCIENCE: What Caused the Attacks

Both attacks happened in dangerous areas where great white sharks hunt. Several divers and kayakers have been attacked by great whites off Pigeon Point, where Omar Conger died. And Paul Parsons was the seventh person to be attacked near Tomales Point in Marin County.

SURF CHAMP MICK FANNING

Date: July 19, 2015
Location: Jeffreys Bay, South Africa

Jeffreys Bay in South Africa is one of the world's best surf spots. It is a dangerous place to surf, though. Beneath the waves swim great white sharks.

JEFFREYS BAY CONTEST

On July 19, 2015, the final of the Jeffreys Bay Open contest was underway. Former world champ Mick Fanning was battling Julian Wilson. The surfers had been in the water for a few minutes. Julian had just caught a wave. Mick was sitting alone on his board about 65 feet (20 m) from shore.

THE ATTACK

Suddenly, a shark's fin appeared behind Mick. He turned around and the shark began to thrash its tail. It hit Mick in the face, knocking him away from his board. At that moment a wave rose up and blocked the view of everyone watching from the shore. All that the spectators could see was splashing from behind the wave. Most people feared the water was about to turn red with blood.

Mick and Julian are picked up by jet skis. Julian had seen the attack and was paddling toward Mick to help.

MICK'S ESCAPE

Thankfully, when Mick next appeared, he was swimming hard toward shore. Rescue boats and jet skis raced to his rescue. Within seconds, Mick and Julian were safely out of the water.

Mick had done everything possible to save himself. He used his surfboard as a shield. Then he fought back by punching the shark as hard as possible. Once the shark had gone, Mick swam for safety as fast as he could.

SHARK SCIENCE:
WHAT CAUSED THE ATTACKS

Why do great whites attack surfers? Part of the reason is the science of how waves break.

Waves break when they reach shallow water. If the water gets shallow quickly, they break more steeply, which is better for surfing. So the best surfing waves are where deep water suddenly gets shallow.

Great whites like to hunt in exactly this kind of place. They are looking for seals or other prey leaving land.

THE SHARK ATTACK THAT WASN'T

Date: October 30, 2004
Location: Ocean Beach, Whangarei, New Zealand

When four swimmers headed into the sea off Ocean Beach, New Zealand, it was the start of an amazing encounter with local sea life.

SWIMMING WITH DOLPHINS

In the water were Karina Cooper, Helen Slade, lifeguard Rob Howes, and his teenage daughter, Niccy. They were all members of the Whangarei Surf Lifesaving Club, out for a training swim. Suddenly, a **pod** of dolphins raced towards them. As Rob said:

"They were . . . turning tight circles around us, slapping the water with their tails."

One of the dolphins swam straight at Rob and Helen before zooming underneath them. As Rob watched what the dolphin was doing, he was horrified to see a 10-foot (3 m) great white swim past. The shark headed for the other two swimmers.

If a dolphin calf is attacked by a shark, the whole pod tries to protect it.

BOTTLENOSE DOLPHIN AND CALF

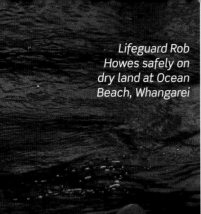

Lifeguard Rob Howes safely on dry land at Ocean Beach, Whangarei

Fending Off the Shark

The dolphins diverted the shark before it could reach the two girls. Then the dolphins swam back and forth around all four humans, forming a protective barrier while the shark kept circling. The humans tread water, and the dolphins stayed with them the whole time. Another lifeguard, Matt Fleet, came over in a boat to see what was going on. He dove in to join the swimmers before seeing the shark. Finally, after 40 minutes, the shark gave up and swam away.

Shark Science:
What Stopped the Attack

Bottlenose dolphins are not usually hunted by sharks, but baby dolphins are sometimes attacked. This may be why dolphins are known to gang up on sharks and fight them off.

Dolphins have been recorded protecting humans more than once. As well as the Ocean Beach lifeguards, long-distance swimmers and divers have been saved by them. Why they do this is not known.

HOW TO AVOID A SHARK ATTACK

If you do not have a dolphin bodyguard (see pages 24–25), what can you do to avoid being attacked by a shark? Here are 10 tips.

SWIM WITH FRIENDS . . . BUT NOT A DOGGY FRIEND!

Sharks are thought to be less likely to attack large groups of people. However, to a shark the noise of a swimming dog is like a dinner bell because it sounds like an injured fish.

NEVER PEE OR BLEED IN THE WATER

Most shark experts think that pee or blood in the water attracts sharks. They may be able to tell that it is not fish blood, but hunting sharks will still come to investigate.

CHECK OUT THE LOCAL HISTORY

If you're in a place where sharks have attacked before, they are probably still out there. Stay out of the water!

AVOID SUDDEN DROP-OFFS, RIVER MOUTHS, AND CHANNELS

Great whites like to hunt in places where shallow water suddenly gets deep (see page 23). Bull sharks haunt river mouths and deeper channels where the water flow may bring them fish and other food.

 AVOID NIGHTTIME . . . AND DAWN . . . AND DUSK!

Sharks hunt mostly at night, but are also active at dawn and dusk. That makes these really bad times to surf/swim/dive.

 BUY A SHARK SCARER, POSSIBLY . . .

Shark scarers use an electric pulse to ward off an attacking shark. (At least one person has been bitten while wearing one, though . . .)

DON'T SWIM IN MURKY WATER

There is less chance of you spotting a shark in murky water and more chance of a small shark bumping into you and biting to see what you are.

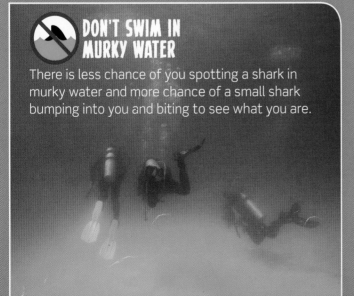

BE VERY CAREFUL ABOUT SPEARFISHING

Many shark attacks have been triggered by fish wriggling on the end of a diver's spear.

WATCH THE SHARK

If a shark does appear, try to keep sight of it. Most sharks prefer to make a surprise attack on their victims.

FIGHT BACK

Many survivors report that they fought back. Shark noses, gills, and eyes are especially sensitive—though they have the disadvantage of being very close to the shark's mouth.

SEVEN INCREDIBLE SHARK FACTS

1 THE UNITED STATES IS TOP OF THE SHARK ATTACK LEAGUE . . .

The United State's first shark attack happened in 1642, when Antony Van Corlear was attacked off Manhattan. From then until the end of 2016, the United States had 1,657 shark attacks, 144 of them fatal.

2 . . . BUT AUSTRALIA'S SHARKS ARE DEADLIER

Australia is second to the United States in total shark attacks, with 904 between 1791 and 2016. An attack in Australia, though, is likely to be more serious. In almost one third of attacks (29 percent), the victim died.

3 SHARKS ATTACK IN UNEXPECTED PLACES

Countries such as the United States, Australia, and South Africa (third in the shark attack league) are known for dangerous sharks. Attacks also happen in more surprising places, such as Italy (10 fatal attacks), South Korea (6), Iraq (3), Turkey (2), and even Russia (4 non-fatal attacks).

4 MOST SHARK ATTACK VICTIMS ARE SURFERS

Surfers are more likely than anyone else to be attacked by a shark. In 2010, for example, they were the victims in more than half of all shark attacks.

5 THERE ARE LOTS OF SHARKS AT NEW SMYRNA, FLORIDA

The International Shark Attack File says that every swimmer at New Smyrna Beach comes within 10 feet (3 m) of a shark. So it's no wonder that 164 shark attacks were recorded there between 1962 and 2016. Fortunately, many were minor and none was fatal.

6 SHARKS ARE LESS DANGEROUS THAN BUCKETS

In 1996, nearly 11,000 Americans were injured in accidents involving buckets. That same year, 13 Americans were injured by sharks.

7 SHARKS ARE LOSING THE FIGHT

Experts estimate that for every human killed by a shark, roughly 2 million sharks are killed by humans. Most are caught for their fins, which are used in soup, or become trapped accidentally in fishermen's nets.

SHARK ATTACKS: THE CHANCES

By now, you might have decided only to swim at the swimming pool because it sounds as though there are sharks on the prowl looking for human victims at every beach! In reality, the chance of even seeing a shark, let alone being attacked by one, is tiny.

SHARKS VS. BEARS

In the United States, researchers have found that you are twice as likely to be killed by a bear as by a shark.

SURFERS VS. NON-SURFERS

Most people (in 2016, 58 percent) who are attacked by sharks are surfers of some kind. So not being a surfer makes it a lot less likely you will be bitten by a shark.

SHARKS VS. DOGS

One survey found that between 2001 and 2010 you were 33 times as likely to be killed by a dog as by a shark. The chances of being bitten, rather than killed, by a dog were even higher.

BEING BITTEN BY A SHARK VS. DROWNING

Based on statistics from the year 2000, the chances of being bitten by a shark that year were 1 in 11.5 million. You would be really unlucky to be that one person out of 11.5 million. Meanwhile, the chances of drowning were 1 in 3.5 million.

SHARKS VS. SAND

Between 1990 and 2006, one-and-a-half times as many Americans were killed by sand holes they had dug collapsing on top of them as by sharks.

In fact, there are a lot of VERY unlikely things that are still more likely to kill you than a shark: a plane crash, a train crash, a cycling accident, fireworks, heat exposure, falling over . . . even death by accidental poisoning is more likely.

GLOSSARY

abalone
shellfish that is prized for its taste

bumped
being nudged or butted by a shark's snout

cage diving
observing sharks underwater from inside a metal cage, which protects the diver from attack

leash
strong, stretchy cord that attaches a surfer's leg to their surfboard

netted
protected by a long net hanging down in the water, which traps dangerous sharks before they get close to shore

perpetrator
someone who does something illegal or harmful to others

pod
group of dolphins or whales

surf mat
small inflatable mat, about 3 feet (1 m) long and 1 foot 6 inches (0.5 m) wide

tourniquet
cord or bandage tied tightly around an arm or leg to stop it from bleeding

INDEX

ABOUT THE AUTHOR

Paul Mason is a prolific author of children's books, many award-nominated, on such subjects as 101 ways to save the planet, vile things that go wrong with the human body, and the world's looniest inventors. Many take off via surprising, unbelievable or just plain revolting facts. Today, he lives at a secret location on the coast of Europe, where his writing shack usually smells of drying wetsuit (he's a former international swimmer and a keen surfer).

Picture Credits